SONG OF CREATION

Song _of_ Creation

SAINT FRANCIS OF ASSISI

LAUGHING ELEPHANT BOOKS MM

ISBN 1-883211-34-4

FIRST PRINTING
ALL RIGHTS RESERVED PRINTED IN SINGAPORE

LAUGHING ELEPHANT

POST OFFICE BOX 4399 SEATTLE WASHINGTON 98104

O most high, almighty, good Lord God, to Thee belong praise, glory, honour, and all blessing!

Praised be my Lord God with all His creatures; and specially our brother the sun, who brings us the day, and who brings us the light; fair is he, and shining with a very great splendour: O Lord, to us he signifies Thee!

Praised be my Lord for our sister the moon,

and for the stars, the which He has set clear and
lovely in heaven.

Praised be my Lord for our brother the wind,

and for air and cloud, calms and all weather, by the which Thou upholdest in life all creatures.

Praised be my Lord for our sister water, who is very serviceable unto us, and humble, and precious, and clean.

Praised be my Lord for our brother fire, through whom Thou givest us light in the darkness; and he is bright and pleasant, and very mighty, and strong.

Praised be my Lord for our mother the earth, the

which doth sustain us and keep us,

and bringeth forth divers fruits,

and flowers of many colours,

and grass.

Praised be my Lord for all those who pardon

one another for His love's sake,

and who endure weakness and tribulation; blessed
are they who peaceably shall endure,

for Thou, O most Highest, shalt give them a crown!

Praised be my Lord for our sister, the death of the body, from whom no man escapeth. Woe to him who dieth in mortal sin! Blessed are they who are found walking by Thy most holy will, for the second death shall have no power to do them harm.

Praise ye, and bless ye the Lord, and give thanks unto Him, and serve Him with great humility.

PICTURE CREDITS

PICTURE CREDITS